1|26|10

100

things you should know about

SAVING
THE EARTH

100

things you should know about

SAVING
THE EARTH

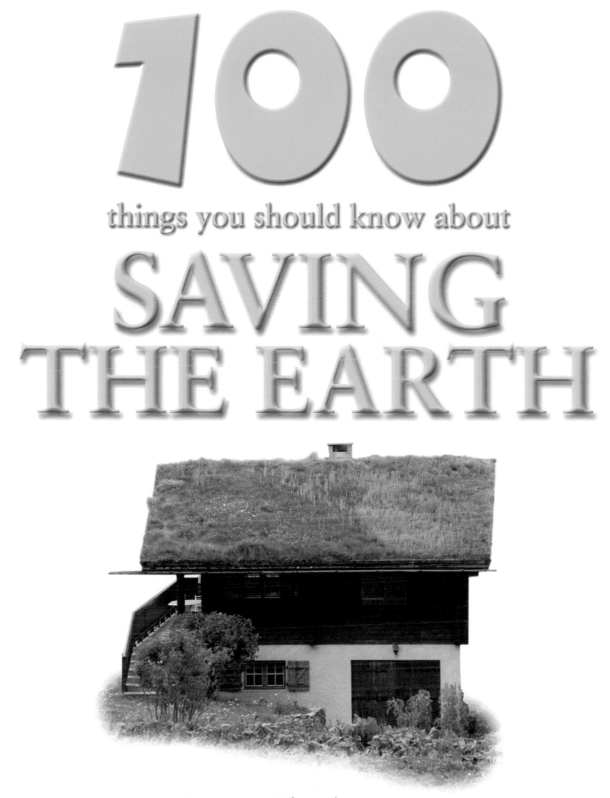

Anna Claybourne
Consultant: Steve Parker

This 2009 edition published and distributed by:
Mason Crest Publishers Inc.
370 Reed Road, Broomall, Pennsylvania 19008
(866) MCP-BOOK (toll free)
www.masoncrest.com

Library of Congress Cataloging-in-Publication data is available
100 Things You Should Know About Saving the Earth
ISBN 978-1-4222-1526-5

100 Things You Should Know About - 10 Title Series
ISBN 978-1-4222-1517-3

Printed in the United States of America

First published as hardback in 2008 by Miles Kelly Publishing Ltd
Bardfield Centre, Great Bardfield, Essex, CM7 4SL

Copyright © Miles Kelly Publishing Ltd 2008

ACKNOWLEDGEMENTS
The publishers would like to thank the following artists
who have contributed to this book:
Julian Baker, Mike Foster
All other artworks are from the Miles Kelly Artwork Bank

The publishers would like to thank the following sources
for the use of their photographs:
Page 6 NASA/Reuters/Corbis; 8 Tui de Roy/Minden Pictures/FLPA;
11 (c) Bettmann/Corbis, (b) schaltwerk.de/Fotolia.com; 12 Tom Uhlman/Alamy;
13 China Photos/Stringer/Getty Images; 14 (b) Klaus Hackenberg/zefa/Corbis;
16 (t) Jean-Paul Pelissier/Reuters/Corbis; 17 (t) Dean Conger/Corbis, (b) Getty Images; 19 www.firebox.com;
20 Arctic-Images/Corbis; 21 (cr) Sunshine Solar Ltd, (bl) Gideon Mendel/Corbis;
22 Victor Habbick Visions/Science Photo Library; 23 Olivier Maire/eps/Corbis, (tl) Phil Schermeister/Corbis;
24 Yann Arthus - Bertrand/Corbis, (bl) Vivianne Moos/Corbis; 26 Gene Blevins/LA Daily News/Corbis;
27 (b) Ron Sanford/Corbis; 28 David Kesti/Fotolia.com; 30 (t) AGStockUSA, Inc./Alamy, (b) Ed Young/Corbis;
31 (t) www.ecozone.co.uk, (b) Ulrich Niehoff/Imagebroker/FLPA;
32 (t) Mike Segar/Reuters/Corbis, (b) Desmond Boylan/Reuters/Corbis; 33 (t) Martin Harvey/Corbis;
34 (t) Steve Estvanik/Fotolia.com, (b) Per-Anders Pettersson; 35 (t) Olga Alexandrova/Fotolia.com;
36 (b) Ennoy Engelhardt/Fotolia.com; 37 (t) Brian S. Turner/Frank Lane Picture Agency/Corbis;
38 (b) Katherine Feng/Globio/Minden Pictures/FLPA; 39 (c) Kate Davidson/epa/Corbis;
41 (tl) Dimas Ardian/Stringer/Getty Images; 42 (b) MiklG/Fotolia.com; 43 (main) Neil Farrin/JAI/Corbis;
43 (t) Jeffrey L Rotman/Corbis; 45 (t) Reuters/Corbis, (c) Yann Arthus-Bertrand/Corbis; 46 Frans Lanting/Corbis

All other photographs are from:
Corel, digitalSTOCK, digitalvision, iStockphoto.com, John Foxx,
PhotoAlto, PhotoDisc, PhotoEssentials, PhotoPro, Stockbyte

Contents

1 **Our planet is in a mess!** Humans have done more damage to the Earth than any other species. We take over land for farms, cities and roads, we hunt animals until they die out and we produce waste and pollution. Gases from cars, power stations, and factories are changing the atmosphere and making the planet heat up. By making a few changes to live in a "greener" way, we can try to save our planet.

99

Being green is a job for everyone. At home, switching off lights and saving water helps to save the Earth. Towns, communities and businesses can help, too, by arranging recycling collections, or banning plastic bags. Governments are already starting to pass laws to limit things such as pollution, logging and overfishing.

100

Planet Earth is the only home we have. It's also the only home for wild animals and plants. After us, it will be the home of future generations. What we do now will decide whether it ends up a messy, overheated planet, or one that's healthy and safe to live on.

Index

Entries in **bold** refer to main subject entries. Entries in *italics* refer to illustrations.

As pollution makes the Earth warm up, more powerful storms form over the sea. This satellite photo shows Hurricane Frances moving over the Caribbean in 2004.

Global warming

Some heat gets trapped by the layer of gases

Sun

Some heat escapes back into space

Layer of gases

Global warming happens when greenhouse gases collect in the Earth's atmosphere. They let heat from the Sun through, but as it bounces back, it gets trapped close to the Earth, making the planet heat up.

2 Throughout its history, the Earth has warmed up and cooled down. Experts think that today's warming is due to humans – and it's happening faster than normal. Carbon dioxide and methane gases are released into the air as pollution. They are known as greenhouse gases and can stop the Sun's heat escaping from the atmosphere.

3 Global warming means that the climate is changing. Weather changes every day – we have hot days and cold days – but on average the climate is warming up. Scientists think that average temperatures have risen by one degree Celsius in the last 100 years, and that they will keep rising.

I DON'T BELIEVE IT!

Scientists think that sea levels could rise by 3 feet by 2100 – maybe even more. Three million years ago when the Earth was hotter, the sea was more than 650 feet higher than today. We could be heading that way again.

4 Warmer temperatures mean wilder weather. Wind happens when air is heated and gets lighter. It rises up and cold air is sucked in to replace it. Rain occurs when heat makes water in rivers and seas turn into vapor in the air. It rises up and forms rain clouds. Warmer temperatures mean more wind, rain, and storms.

The ice in the Arctic Ocean is melting so fast that scientists think over half of it could be gone by 2100.

ARCTIC OCEAN

KEY

Average area of sea covered by ice from 1980–2000

Predicted area of sea covered by ice for 2080–2100

Huge chunks of ice often break off into the sea at Paradise Bay, at the Antarctic.

As the Earth heats up, its ice melts. Vast areas of the Earth are covered in ice. It is found around the North and South Poles, and on high mountains. Now, because of global warming, more and more of this ice is melting. It turns into water and flows into the sea. Also, as the water gets warmer, it expands (gets bigger) and the sea takes up more space, making sea levels rise.

Polar bears depend on large chunks of ice to hunt and rest on. Melting ice in the Arctic is making life much harder for them.

9

Energy crisis

6 We pump greenhouse gases into the atmosphere because we burn fuels to make energy. Cars, planes, and trains run on fuel, and we also burn it in power stations to produce electricity. The main fuels – coal, oil, and gas – are called fossil fuels because they formed underground over millions of years.

Oil and natural gas formed from the remains of tiny prehistoric sea creatures that collected on the seabed. Layers of rock built up on top and squashed them. Over time, they became underground stores of oil, with pockets of gas above.

7 Fossil fuels are running out. Because they take so long to form, we are using up fossil fuels much faster than they can be replaced. Eventually, they will become so rare that it will be too expensive to find them. Experts think this will happen before the end of the 21st century.

Oil platform drilling for oil and gas

Hard rock layer

Gas

Oil

Oil and gas move upwards through soft rock layers until reaching a hard rock layer

The layer of dead sea creatures is crushed by rock that forms above, and turns into oil and gas

Tiny sea creatures die and sink to the seabed

QUIZ

Which of these things are used to supply electricity?
A. Burning coal B. Wind
C. The flow of rivers
D. Hamsters on wheels E. Sunshine
F. The energy of earthquakes

Answers:
A, B, C and E. Hamsters could turn tiny turbines, but would make very little electricity. Earthquakes contain vast amounts of energy, but we have not found a way to harness it.

8 One thing we can do is find other fuels. Besides fossil fuels, we can burn fuels that come from plants. For example, the rape plant contains oil that can be burned in vehicle engines. However, burning these fuels still releases greenhouse gases.

9 Nuclear power is another kind of energy.

By splitting apart atoms – the tiny units that all materials are made of – energy is released, which can be turned into electricity. However, producing this energy creates toxic waste that can make people ill, and may be accidentally released into the air. Safer ways to use nuclear power are being researched.

10 Lots of energy is produced without burning anything.

Hydroelectric power stations use the pushing power of flowing rivers to turn turbines. Hydroelectricity is a renewable, or green, energy source – it doesn't use anything up or cause pollution. Scientists are also working on ways to turn the movement of waves and tides into usable energy.

The Grand Coulee Dam in Washington, USA, holds back a river, creating a lake, or reservoir. Water is let through the dam to turn turbines, which create electricity.

11 The wind and the Sun are great renewable sources of energy, too.

Wind turbines turn generators, which convert the "turning movement" into electricity. Solar panels work by collecting sunlight and turning it into an electrical current.

Solar panels are made of materials that soak up sunlight and turn its energy into a flow of electricity.

Rotor blade

Modern wind turbines usually have three blades, which spin around at speed in high winds.

On the move

12 **Cars release a lot of greenhouse gases.** No one had a car 200 years ago. Now, there are around 500 million cars in the world and most are used daily. Cars burn gasoline or diesel, which are made from oil – a fossil fuel. We can reduce greenhouse gases and slow down global warming by using cars less.

In many cities, there are so many cars that they cause big traffic jams. They move slowly with their engines running, churning out even more pollution.

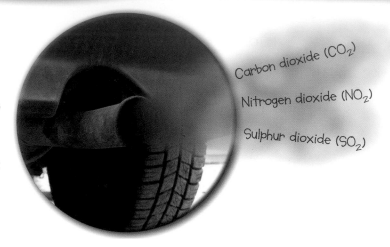

Carbon dioxide (CO_2)

Nitrogen dioxide (NO_2)

Sulphur dioxide (SO_2)

Car exhaust fumes contain harmful, polluting gases, including sulphur dioxide, nitrogen dioxide and carbon dioxide, which are poisonous to humans.

13 **Public transport is made up of buses, trams and trains that everyone can use.** It's a greener way to travel than by car. Buses can carry 60 or 70 people at once and trains can carry several hundred. They still burn fuel, but release much less greenhouse gases per person.

COUNT YOUR STEPS

Besides saving on greenhouse gases, walking is great exercise and helps you stay healthy. Try counting your steps for one whole day. How many can you do – 3,000, 5,000 or even 10,000?

14 Planes fly long distances at high speeds, giving out tons of greenhouse gases on each journey. A flight from the USA to Europe releases more carbon dioxide than a car does in one year. Where you can, travel by boat or train for shorter journeys.

Maglev trains use magnets to hover above the rails. The magnetic force propels the train forward, rather than a gasoline- or diesel-burning engine.

Cyclists in Beijing, China, enjoy World Car-Free Day. This was organized to help reduce pollution.

This graph shows the world's top ten producers of carbon-based pollution (including carbon dioxide – a major greenhouse gas). These figures are based on emissions in 2004.

CO_2 emissions (millions of tons)

6000
5000
4000
3000
2000
1000
0

USA China Russia India Japan Germany Canada UK North Korea Italy

15 The greenest way to get around is to walk. For short journeys, walk instead of going by car. Inside buildings, use the stairs instead of taking lifts and escalators. Cycling is good, too. A bicycle doesn't burn any fuels, it just uses the power of your legs.

16 Long ago, before engines and turbines were invented, transport worked differently. Boats had sails or oars and were driven by wind or human power, and carts and carriages were pulled by animals. As fossil fuels run out, we may see some old means of transportation coming back.

Save energy at home

17 **Saving electricity at home reduces pollution.** Most electricity we use is produced from burning fossil fuels. By using less of it, we can cut greenhouse gas emissions. Always turn off lights, TVs, computers and other electrical devices when not in use. Low-energy light bulbs are a good idea, too. They use less power and last longer.

19 **We invent all kinds of electrical gadgets to do things for us, but do we really need them?** You can save energy by sweeping the floor instead of using a vacuum cleaner every time. Use your hands to make bread, instead of a food processor. Avoid electrical can openers, knives and other power-hungry gadgets.

Washing hung outside dries in the heat of the Sun. This saves on electricity and fossil fuels.

18 **Your washing can be green as well as clean!** Tumble dryers dry quickly, but they use lots of electricity. In summer, peg your clothes out on a washing line in the garden. In winter, hang them on a drier close to a radiator. You can save even more energy by washing clothes at a lower temperature, such as 86°F.

I DON'T BELIEVE IT!

Only 10 percent of the electricity used by an old-style light bulb is turned into light. The rest turns into wasted heat, which also makes it burn out quicker.

20

Solar panels are a green way to power a home. They work the same way that solar-powered calculators do – they can change sunlight into electricity straight away. If a home produces more electricity than it needs, it can sell some back to the local energy provider.

Solar panels are often made of silicon. When sunlight hits the silicon, electrical charges can flow as an electrical current.

Sunlight

Sunlight

Solar panels can be installed on rooftops to provide power for homes.

Growing turf on the roof is a good way to insulate a house to prevent heat from escaping and being wasted. The grass uses up CO_2, and makes oxygen, too.

Wires carry the flow of electricity to appliances, such as lights

Solar panel

21

Turn down the heating in your house and keep warm in other ways! If you're cold put on an extra sweater, or wrap up warm under a cosy blanket or quilt. You will also save energy if your home has insulation in the walls and roof, and double-glazed windows.

Green shopping

22 **Most people buy something from a shop every day.** Items such as food, clothes and furniture take a lot of energy to grow, manufacture and then transport to the shops. By doing some smart shopping, you can save some of that energy.

Old plastic bags fill up landfill sites and take hundreds of years to rot away. They can also harm wildlife.

Bags made from cloth can be used over and over again.

23 **Say no to plastic bags!** Plastic bags are made from oil – a fossil fuel – and it takes energy to make them. However, we often use them once then throw them away, which creates litter and pollution. When you go shopping take a re-usable bag made from cloth, or re-use old plastic bags so that you don't have to use new ones.

24
How far has your food travelled? The distance food has been transported is called 'food miles'. You can reduce food miles by shopping at farm shops and local markets. In supermarkets, look at packages to find food that was produced nearby. Food that has travelled far is greener if it came by boat, and not by plane.

On the island of Saint Vincent in the Caribbean, people buy bananas that have been grown locally. Bananas grown here are also shipped to other countries — a much greener way to transport than by plane.

25
More and more people are buying bottled water. Water is heavy and a lot of fuel is needed to transport it long distances. The plastic bottles create waste and cause pollution, too. It's greener to use clean, pure water from the tap at home.

26
Buying second-hand goods is a great way to save energy. When you buy second-hand clothes, furniture or books nothing new has to be made in a factory. Antique furniture and vintage clothes are often better quality than new things and more individual, too.

This paper shows that anything can be recycled! Roo Poo paper is made from 80 percent recycled paper and 20 percent kangaroo droppings.

Reduce, re-use, recycle

27 **Most of us buy more than we need.** We want the latest clothes, toys and cars even though we may not need them – this is called consumerism. Reduce, re-use, and recycle is a good way to remember what we can do to reduce the amount of things we buy.

28 **To start with, reduce your shopping.** Do you or your family ever buy things that don't end up getting used? Next time, think before you buy – be sure that you are going to use it. Buying less means less things have to be made, transported, and thrown away. It saves money, too!

Recycling materials greatly reduces the amount of energy needed to make new products. This graph shows how much energy is saved in making new products using recycled materials, rather than raw materials.

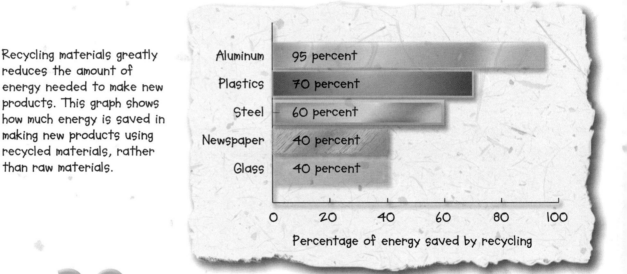

	Percentage of energy saved by recycling	
Aluminum	95 percent	
Plastics	70 percent	
Steel	60 percent	
Newspaper	40 percent	
Glass	40 percent	

0   20   40   60   80   100

Percentage of energy saved by recycling

Empty glass bottles go into a recycling bin.

29 **Recycling means that materials can be made into new things instead of thrown away.** This saves energy and makes less waste. Paper, cardboard, food cans, glass, and some plastics can all be recycled. Some towns and cities collect them, or you can take them to a recycling collection point at a school, supermarket, or dump.

The bottles are collected from the recycling bin and transported to a glass recycling plant.

The old, broken glass is cleaned and melted down with other substances.

I DON'T BELIEVE IT!

Many things we buy are built to break easily. This is called "built-in obsolescence." Manufacturers hope that when your things break, you'll buy new ones from them.

30

We live in a "throwaway society." We are used to disposable things that get used once, then go in the garbage. When something breaks, it's easy to get another, but making and transporting these new things uses up raw materials, and creates pollution. Re-use some of the things you throw away – mend clothes by sewing on a new button, pocket, or patch, and use empty food containers to store things in.

These shopping bags have been made from old, recycled food sacks. They save on raw materials and cut down on plastic bags.

31

If you can't re-use something yourself, maybe someone else can. Give old clothes, furniture, books and toys to a charity shop, or sell them at a car boot sale or a fundraising sale at school.

The bottles are sold and used, and can then be recycled again.

Recycled glass is used in road surfaces, concrete production, and a finely ground glass is used to fill golf bunkers. New bottles and jars are also made from recycled glass.

The bottles are filled with drinks and labeled.

The liquid glass is blow moulded (blown with air) into new bottles.

Green machines

32 As well as using machines less, we can use greener ones. Cars, computers and electrical appliances don't have to use lots of energy. Scientists are working on greener versions that use less electricity or fuel – or even none at all.

33 When hydrogen gas burns, it doesn't release any greenhouse gases – just water. Today, some cars run on hydrogen and create no pollution. However, making the hydrogen for them to run on uses up electricity, and in turn fossil fuels. As fossil fuels run out and renewable energy sources take over, hydrogen cars may become common.

I DON'T BELIEVE IT!

The fastest human-powered vehicles are recumbent cycles, which the rider drives in a lying-down position. They can travel at over 80 miles per hour.

A hydrogen-powered car and a hydrogen fuel station show what more of us could be using in the future.

Hydrogen
Fuel station Vetnisstöð

HYDROGEN
GM
GM FUEL CELL TECHNOLOGY

HYDROGEN3

34 You might have travelled on an electric train or bus before. Instead of burning fuel, they run on electricity supplied from a large, on-board battery or overhead cables. This means less air pollution in city centres.

Trams like this can be found in many cities around the world. They work by collecting electricity from overhead wires or cables.

35 Did you know that "white goods" can be green? White goods are refrigerators, washing machines, dishwashers and other kitchen appliances. New ones have a rating showing how green they are. The greenest ones use the least energy and supplies such as water. Now you can choose the best ones for the planet.

This solar-powered phone charger uses solar panels to turn sunlight into an electricity supply.

As well as saving on electricity, wind-up radios are very useful in parts of the world where there is no electricity supply, such as parts of Africa.

36 Wind-up power was once used for toys, but now there are wind-up radios, flashlights, and cell phone chargers. The handle is wound and the energy from this movement is turned into an electricity supply inside the machine. Wind-up machines save on fossil fuels and reduce greenhouse gases.

Science solutions

An artist's impression of a space shield that could be used to shade the Earth from the Sun.

37 Using less energy is one way to slow down global warming, but there might be others, too. Scientists are coming up with all kinds of space-age and hi-tech solutions that could help the Earth to cool down again.

38 Maybe we could shade the Earth to cool it down. Scientists have lots of ideas about how to do this. Some of these include launching huge mirrors into space to reflect the Sun's light and heat away, or filling the atmosphere with tiny particles to blot out the Sun. Another is to spread out a fine mesh, like a giant sheet, into space to make a sunshade. So far, all of these ideas are far too expensive to try.

I DON'T BELIEVE IT!

In a single day a cow can give out 132 gallons of methane gas. That's enough to fill more than 100 party balloons!

A huge cloud of green algae can be seen near the shore of Lake Tahoe, between California and Nevada. Algae is made up of millions of tiny plants. There is so much algae in the world that it soaks up a lot of the world's carbon dioxide.

39 Instead of greenhouse gases filling the air, we could soak them up. Plants naturally take in carbon dioxide (CO_2) – a greenhouse gas – so planting lots of trees helps to slow global warming. Scientists are also trying to develop special types of algae (tiny plants) that can soak up even more greenhouse gases.

Sunlight

Sugars (food for the plant)

Water

CO_2

Oxygen

Plants make food using sunlight, by a process called photosynthesis. They use up carbon dioxide and give out oxygen.

40 We could catch greenhouse gases before they escape into the air. There are already devices that can do this, which capture carbon dioxide from power stations and factory chimneys. Once it is caught, the gas needs to be stored safely. Scientists are looking at ways of storing carbon dioxide, or changing it into something harmless.

A special foam wrapping is unrolled over the Tortin glacier in Switzerland to stop it melting.

41 As they digest grass, cows and other grazing animals pass a lot of wind! This gas contains methane – a greenhouse gas. Besides burning fuels, this is one of the biggest causes of global warming. Scientists are experimenting with feeding cows different foods to reduce the amount of methane.

Pollution problems

42 **Pollution means dirt, waste, and other substances that damage our surroundings.** Our farms and factories often release harmful chemicals into rivers and lakes, and cars, trucks, and other road vehicles give out poisonous, polluting gases. Litter and garbage are pollution, too.

A thick layer of smog hangs over the city of Bangkok, the capital of Thailand.

43 **Humans make waste — when we go to the toilet.** The waste and water from our toilets is called sewage. This usually ends up at sewage works where we process it to make it safe, but in some places sewage flows straight into rivers or the sea. It is smelly and dirty and can contain deadly germs.

44 **Pollution can harm our health.** Smog is a mixture of smoke from factories and motor vehicles, and fog, and it collects over some cities. It makes it harder to breathe, worsening illnesses such as asthma.

People in Kuala Lumpur, the capital of Malaysia, wear masks to avoid breathing in smog.

People who live near airports have to put up with the sound of low-flying planes flying over their houses.

45

Even noise is a kind of pollution. Noise from airports disturbs the people who live nearby, and loud noises from ships and submarines can disturb whales. They rely on their own sounds to find their way and send messages, so other noises can confuse them.

46

The more we throw away, the more garbage piles up. When we drop garbage just anywhere, it becomes litter. If we put garbage in a trash can, some of it may get recycled, and the rest gets taken away and dumped in a big hole in the ground, called a landfill site. Either way, there's too much of it!

At landfill sites, garbage piles up making huge mountains of waste that have to be flattened down by rollers.

47

Air pollution can cause acid rain. The waste gases from power stations and factories mix with water droplets in clouds and form weak acid. This makes soil, rivers and lakes more acidic, which can kill fish and plants. Acid rain can even make rock crumble and dissolve.

TRUE OR FALSE?

1. Garbage isn't a problem if you put it in a garbage can.
2. Acid rain can make your nose fall off.
3. Loud noises make whales get lost.

Answers:
1. FALSE – it still piles up in landfill sites. 2. FALSE – the acid is not very strong, but it can dissolve away the stone nose of a statue. 3. TRUE – according to some scientists.

Litter and rubbish

48 After leaving your house, garbage has a long life ahead of it. Things such as banana skins will rot away quickly, but man-made products such as plastics take a long time to decay and break down. That's why landfill sites fill up fast, and we have to find more and more space for our garbage.

Forest fires caused by dropped litter, such as glass bottles and cigarette ends, can be deadly and cost a lot of money to put out. Here, a helicopter drops water onto a forest fire.

49 A drinks bottle left in a dry field or forest could start a fire. The curved glass in a bottle – especially a piece of a broken bottle – can act like a magnifying glass. If it focuses the Sun's heat on a dry patch of grass, a fire can start.

I DON'T BELIEVE IT!

People drop the most litter from cars because they think they can make a quick getaway! However, governments are making new laws to stop littering from cars.

Leaving your junk in a public place is known as littering. Mattresses, tires and shopping carts are often dumped in the countryside.

50
Some people treat the countryside and other public places as a dumping ground. Big items, such as mattresses, sofas, and shopping carts, are sometimes dumped on roadsides or in rivers. Besides looking a mess, these things can release poisons as they rot away.

51
The plastic rings that hold cans together can be deadly for wildlife. These stretchy loops are used to hold drinks cans together in packs. As litter, they can get caught around the neck of a wild animal, such as a seagull, and strangle it. Snip the loops open with scissors before throwing them away.

Fishing nets left on beaches can endanger wildlife. This one has become tangled around a sea lion's neck.

Ducks struggle through a pond polluted with plastic bottles.

52
Fishing weights and lines left near rivers and lakes can choke or strangle water wildlife. Weights sometimes contain lead and this can poison water birds, such as swans. People who go fishing should make sure they never leave any of their equipment behind.

Reducing waste

53 There are lots of things you can do to reduce waste. When you throw something away, think if it could be recycled or re-used instead. Avoid buying things that will have to be thrown away after one use.

MAKE SOME COMPOST

Make a heap of plant waste, fruit and vegetable skins, and grass cuttings in a corner of your garden. It takes a few months to turn into compost. To help it along, mix it around and dig it over with a garden fork. When the compost is ready, you can use it for potting plants or add it to soil in your garden.

You can buy a specially made compost bin to make compost in, like this one.

54 Instead of throwing away fruit and vegetable peelings, turn them into compost. When your peelings rot down, they turn into a rich, fertile soil that's great for your garden. All you need is a space outside where you can pile up your waste for composting, or you can get a special compost bin.

The composting process

① Waste, including fruit and vegetable peelings, tea bags, leaves, and eggshells, goes in the top.

② Tiny organisms called microbes start to break down the waste, which makes it heat up.

③ Insects help to break it down even more and worms help air to get into the compost.

④ The compost is brown and moist and should smell earthy.

55

Millions of disposable batteries end up in landfill sites every year. They take a long time to decay and when they do, they release harmful chemicals. Rechargeable batteries can be refilled with energy from the mains and re-used many times.

56

Reduce your waste – pick re-usables, not disposables. Face wipes and disposable diapers, cups and cooking trays are all things that we use once, then throw away. It's greener to use re-useables, such as washable baking trays, cloth dish towels, and washable diapers.

57

Lots of the things we buy come wrapped up several times over. We take them home, unwrap them, and throw the packaging away. Choose products with less packaging, or none at all.

Much of our rubbish is made up of pointless packaging that we don't really need.

TIME TO DECOMPOSE

Fruit and vegetables	2 days to 6 months
Newspaper	6 months
Drinks cans	100 to 500 years
Disposable diapers	200 to 500 years
Plastic bags	450 years
Plastic bottles	100 to 1000 years +

This tractor is spraying chemicals onto crops to kill pests and weeds. When it rains the chemicals wash into rivers and can harm wildlife.

58 **Big companies need to cut the pollution they produce.** There are laws to ban them dumping toxic chemicals and to limit dangerous waste gases, but they're not yet tough enough to make a big difference. Pressure groups such as Greenpeace are fighting for stronger, better laws.

This tractor is using a different method — cutting back weeds between the crops, instead of spraying them. This keeps the environment cleaner.

59 **Weedkillers and insect sprays kill unwanted plants and bugs in the garden.** However, because they are poisonous they can kill other wildlife too, and cause pollution. It's greener to pull up weeds and pick off pests instead.

60 Cleaning your house can make the planet dirty! Strong cleaning chemicals that are washed down the sink can end up in water supplies. Try to use less of them, or use natural, home-made alternatives. A mixture of water and vinegar is great for cleaning windows.

Some companies are now making re-useable washing balls that clean clothes without using any detergent.

61 Paint, paint stripper and varnish contain toxic chemicals. These chemicals don't break down naturally when they are poured away, which results in pollution. If you can, save them to use again, or see if your local council will collect them for re-using (some councils do this).

62 Shampoo, face creams and make-up are full of polluting chemicals. Pick greener products that contain natural ingredients. You can even use everyday ingredients, such as olive oil, to make your own skin treatments.

Soap nuts are berries of the soapberry tree. They contain a natural, soapy chemical that can be used to wash clothes.

MAKE A FOOT SOAK

Mix together:
1 tablespoon of fine oatmeal
1 tablespoon of skimmed milk powder
1 teaspoonful of dried rosemary

Spoon the mixture into an old, clean sock and tie a knot at the top. Leave the sock in a bowl of warm water for a few minutes, then soak your feet in the water for 20 minutes.

Wildlife in danger

Wild animals, such as leopards and tigers, are still killed for their fur to make items such as handbags and rugs.

63 Since humans have existed on Earth, many living things have been destroyed. To make space for cities, farms, and roads, people have taken over wild areas, and plants and animals have lost their natural homes, or habitats. This is called habitat loss and it is the main reason why wildlife is in danger.

64 Toxic waste, oil spills, and pesticides can be deadly for wildlife. In the 1950s, a chemical called DDT was used to kill insects on crops, but it affected other animals including wild birds. It made them lay eggs with very thin shells that cracked easily. The birds began to die out as they could not have chicks.

This bird is covered in oil spilt from an oil tanker (a ship that carries oil). If birds like this aren't cleaned, they will die.

These nature reserve wardens in Dzanga-Ndoki National Park in the Central African Republic have caught some poachers hunting protected animals.

65
Wild plants and animals suffer when we exploit them – use them to meet our needs. Humans hunt wild animals for their skins, meat, and other body parts, such as ivory from elephants' tusks. Some people steal wild plants, too. If too many are taken, their numbers fall fast.

QUIZ

What do these words mean?
1. Extinct 2. Species
3. Endangered 4. Habitat

Answers:
1. Died out and no longer existing. 2. A particular type of living thing. 3. In danger of becoming extinct. 4. The surroundings where a plant or animal lives.

66
Human activities have wiped out some species, or types, of living things. When a species no longer exists, it is said to be extinct. The great auk – a large-beaked, black-and-white sea bird – became extinct in the 1850s due to hunting by humans. Many other species are now close to extinction, including the tiger and mountain gorilla.

The orangutan – a type of ape – is an extremely threatened species, and one of our closest animal cousins.

67
When a creature is in danger of becoming extinct, we call it threatened. Severely threatened species are known as endangered. These labels help to teach people about the dangers to wildlife. They also help us to make laws to try to protect these species from hunters and collectors.

Saving habitats

68 **To save wildlife, we need to save habitats.** Humans are taking up more and more space and if we don't slow down, there'll be no wild, natural land left. We need to leave plenty of natural areas for wildlife to live in.

These penguins live in Antarctica. Their habitat is ice and freezing water and it could be affected by global warming.

69 **One hundred years ago, people went on safari to hunt animals.** Today, more tourists go to watch wild animals and plants in their natural habitat – this is called ecotourism and it helps wildlife. Local people can make enough money from tourism, so they don't need to hunt. However, ecotourism can disturb wildlife, so tourists have to take care where they go.

Tourists in a jeep approach a pride of lions in a nature reserve in South Africa.

70 **Nature reserves and national parks are safe homes for wildlife.** The land is kept wild and unspoiled to preserve natural habitats. There are also guards or wardens to protect the wildlife and watch out for hunters.

As the human population continues to rise, more and more wild, natural land is being taken over.

71 It can be hard for humans to preserve habitats because we need space too. There are nearly 7 billion (7,000,000,000) humans on Earth today. Experts think this will rise to at least 9 billion. Some countries have laws to limit the number of children people are allowed to have to try to control the population.

A diver explores a coral reef. The corals are home to many species of fish, crabs and shellfish.

72 You can help to keep habitats safe. In the countryside, don't take stones, shells or flowers. Visit nature reserves – your money helps to run them. Don't buy souvenirs made of coral, or other animals or plants, as this encourages hunting and habitat destruction.

I DON'T BELIEVE IT!

The river Thames in London has just 10 percent of the pollution it had in the 1950s because of pollution prevention, and is home to over 100 species of fish.

73 If you have a garden at home or at school, you could make it into a safe place for wildlife to live. Yards and empty lots are parts of towns and cities that can stay wild. They can be a good habitat for many species of small animals and wild plants.

An insect box provides a home for creatures, such as bees and ladybirds.

In some parts of the world, hedgehogs like hiding under leaves.

74 Wild creatures love a messy yard. If yards are always tidy there is nowhere for animals to hide. Leave parts of your yard untidy and overgrown — let grass and weeds grow and don't clear up piles of leaves. These areas provide shelter and homes for spiders, beetles, birds, and squirrels.

FOOD FOR BIRDS

Here are some snacks to try putting out for garden birds:
Grated hard cheese
Raisins
Sunflower seeds or other seeds
Chopped or crushed nuts
Meat scraps
Fresh, chopped coconut

Avoid putting out dry or salty food, such as stale bread or salted nuts, as it's bad for birds.

75 You can help wild birds by feeding them. Feed birds in winter — there are fewer berries and insects for them to eat at this time of year. Put up a bird table, or hang bird feeders from trees in your garden.

Butterflies such as tortoiseshells like to feed on the flowers of a buddleia bush.

A chickadee and a red squirrel are helping themselves to nuts from this bird feeder.

76 Bees and butterflies feed on nectar — a sweet juice found inside flowers. A garden full of flowers will provide lots of food for insects. They especially like sunflowers, lavender, and clover.

Sunflowers are great for wildlife. They provide nectar for insects and nutritious seeds for birds.

77 Thick, thorny bushes are brilliant for birds. Some bushes, such as brambles and hawthorns, provide berries that birds like to eat. Thick, tangled bushes also make safe places for birds to build their nests or hide from animals, such as pet cats.

Saving species

78 Goods made from threatened wildlife species can be bought around the world. Although there are laws to protect plants and animals, they are often broken. It's best not to buy anything that might come from a threatened species, such as ivory, skins, horns or bones.

Parrots are sometimes stolen from the wild as chicks and sold as pets.

80 You or your class could sponsor an endangered animal, such as a tiger. You pay a small fee that goes toward caring for the animal and running the zoo or reserve where it lives. In return, you'll get letters or e-mails about your animal's progress. Zoos and wildlife organizations can help you to do this.

79 Exotic pets can be exciting, but they are sometimes stolen from the wild. Avoid having an unusual pet such as a rare lizard or parrot. It could be a threatened species that has been taken away from its natural habitat.

A Greenpeace ship (far left) encounters a whaling ship, the *Nisshin Maru*, in the Antarctic Ocean. Some countries still hunt whales, but campaigning groups such as Greenpeace are trying to stop it.

I DON'T BELIEVE IT!

Millions of sharks, including threatened species, are hunted every year to make shark's fin soup. The soup is an expensive delicacy in China.

81 People still hunt threatened species, even though it's illegal. Many people in the world are very poor and some can't resist hunting a threatened tiger to sell its skin, or a shark to sell its fins. Governments need to try to reduce poverty, to help wildlife as well as people.

82 To help endangered animals, visit your nearest zoo. Most zoos have captive breeding programs. These help endangered animals to have babies to increase their numbers. Some can then be released back into the wild.

In China, giant pandas are being bred successfully on wildlife reserves. These are just some of the new babies born in recent years.

Forests and farms

83 Every year, over 30 million acres of forests are logged (cut down). That's an area the size of the country of Malawi in Africa, or the US state of Pennsylvania. Trees do grow again, but we are cutting forests down much faster than they can grow back.

This chart shows the reasons for deforestation in the Amazon rainforest.

COLOMBIA

ECUADOR

PERU

BOLIVIA

BRAZIL

Extent of the Amazon rainforest

17.1 percent of the Amazon rainforest has already been destroyed

60 percent   Cattle ranches
30 percent   Small-scale farming
3 percent   Fires, building, roads, dams
7 percent   Other

Over half of the rainforest left in the world is in the Amazon in South America. Nearly one-fifth of the Amazon rainforest has already disappeared.

84 One way to save trees is to re-use wood. Instead of buying brand-new wooden objects and furniture, buy second-hand ones. If you do buy new ones, check that the wood comes from a 'sustainable forest'. This means that the trees are only cut down as fast as they can grow back.

85 Farms take up almost 40 percent of the Earth's land. We need farms to provide us with food – to grow crops and keep animals on – but they have a big impact on the Earth. Most farmland is devoted to one type of crop or animal, so many types of wildlife that live there lose their homes.

Large areas of rainforest in Indonesia and Malaysia have been cut down to make way for oil palm tree plantations. The fruits of the oil palm are harvested for their oil, which can be found in one in ten supermarket products.

86 Organic farming can be a greener way to farm. It doesn't use artificial chemicals, such as pesticides and fertilizers, which means it is good for wildlife and the soil. If you buy organic food and other products, you help to keep the Earth cleaner.

I DON'T BELIEVE IT!

In prehistoric times, forests covered more than half of the Earth's land. Today, almost half of those forests have gone.

87 Buying nuts can help save the rainforests. Some products, such as brazil nuts, grow on rainforest trees. By buying them, you are helping farmers to keep rainforests alive, instead of cutting them down to grow other crops.

As most nuts grow on trees, they are one crop that can be grown without cutting them down.

Seas and coasts

88 Seas and oceans cover the biggest part of the Earth's surface – nearly three-quarters of it! Pollution, global warming, and fishing have a huge effect on the sea and its wildlife.

89 Pollution from farms, factories, and houses often flows into rivers and ends up in the sea. Tiny sea plants and animals absorb the chemicals. When they are eaten by larger sea creatures, the polluting chemicals are passed on from one animal to the next. Many large sea creatures, such as sharks and polar bears, have been found to have a lot of toxic chemicals in their bodies.

90 Coastal areas are in trouble because of rising sea levels. As the sea rises, tides, tsunamis, and storm waves can reach further inland. If the sea rises much more, it could put many coastal cities underwater. The danger of the sea flooding the land is one of the biggest reasons to try to slow down global warming.

In Thailand, signs on beaches and streets give warnings and provide evacuation directions to be used in the event of a tsunami. Thailand is one of the countries that was devastated by the tsunami that struck on December 26, 2004.

91

For thousands of years, humans have hunted fish. Today, we are catching so many fish that some types are in danger of disappearing – this is called overfishing. To try to stop it, there are laws to give fishing boats a quota, or limit, on how many fish they can catch.

Low-lying islands, such as this one in Fiji, are in danger of disappearing as sea levels rise.

Cod is one type of fish that has been overfished in some parts of the world.

92

There's precious treasure in the seabed. It contains oil – a fossil fuel – and many other useful minerals. However, drilling and digging into the seabed damages wildlife and sea habitats, such as coral reefs. Governments are starting to set up nature reserves in the sea, as well as on land. In these areas, no mining or drilling is allowed.

Oil rigs such as this one are built around a giant drill that bores into the seabed to extract oil.

Water resources

93 The world is using too much water.

In many places, water is being pumped out of lakes, rivers and underground wells faster than rain can replace it. As the human population grows, so will the need for water.

Most of the world's freshwater is frozen! The figures below show where the fresh water is found.

Ice caps and glaciers
77.2 percent

Ground water
22.26 percent

Rivers and lakes
0.32 percent

Soil
0.18 percent

Atmosphere
0.04 percent

94 Global warming is causing huge water problems.
Some areas are getting more rain and floods, as hotter temperatures lead to more clouds and storms. Floods often pollute water supplies. Other places are becoming hotter and drier, leading to droughts. Either way, global warming is leading to water shortages.

This boat was left high and dry in the Aral Sea in central Asia, which is shrinking because its water has been drained to water crops.

Villagers in Pakistan collect water from a deep well after a rain shower during a drought.

95 In some countries, drinking water comes from the sea.

Seawater is much too salty to drink, but in dry countries, such as Kuwait, they have factories called desalination plants. They take the salt out of seawater to make it fit to drink. However this process uses up lots of energy and is not a long-term solution.

96 Having a green garden saves water!

Many people pave their gardens over for a patio, but rain flows straight off the hard surface and can lead to floods. If gardens are kept as soil and plants, rain soaks into the ground and keeps water supplies topped up.

An aerial view of a desalination plant in Kuwait.

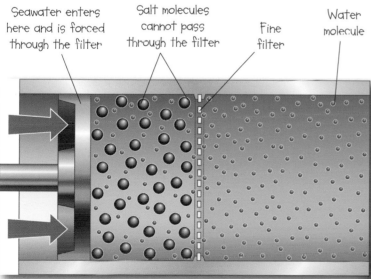

Seawater enters here and is forced through the filter

Salt molecules cannot pass through the filter

Fine filter

Water molecule

The salt is removed from seawater by pushing it through a very fine filter, making it drinkable. This process is called reverse osmosis.

The environment around us

97 The word environment means the place that surrounds us. Planet Earth and all the habitats on it make up our environment. That's why being green is sometimes called environmentalism.

We need to let as much of the Earth as possible stay in its natural state, such as this beautiful forest in Borneo.

98 As this book shows, the Earth is changing too fast. To be green, and to care for the environment, we need to change the Earth as little as possible. We must reduce the litter, pollution and greenhouse gases that we produce. At the same time we must take less away from it.

TURN YOUR SCHOOL GREEN

One thing you can do to help save the Earth is persuade your school to go green (or greener).
Here are some ideas:

• Arrange a recycling rota to collect waste paper from all the classrooms and offices.

• Make posters to put up in the toilets to remind people to save water.

• If there's space, set up a school wildlife garden and compost heap – persuade the kitchen staff to compost food leftovers.